BECOME A YOUTUBE INFLUENCER IN 365 DAYS OR LESS

How to Start a Channel and Generate Passive Income for Beginners

Nicholas Gallo, PT, DPT

Table of Contents

Introduction

I wrote this guide to help people who have aspirations to start an influencial YouTube channel. My story goes like this: I have a Doctorate in Physical Therapy and did NOT go to school for social media marketing. After obtaining my degree, I had only ever used YouTube to look up information on something I was doing or any type of informational purposes. One day, I was approached by a colleague who knew a healthcare provider with a very profitable and successful YouTube channel. Personally, I thought posting YouTube videos would be super difficult and a waste of time. "Oh, that isn't going to work. Why would anyone ever want to watch us on YouTube?" Believe it or not, that is most people's mentality.

After some deliberation, I decided to do a bit of research about the benefits of owning a YouTube channel and the incentives. I discovered that YouTubers can create very profitable channels. The best part? It is passive income! How could people be generating this type of income by literally just filming themselves?

This newfound knowledge made my colleague and I decide that we should meet and discuss the possibility of creating a YouTube channel dedicated to physical therapy-related content. As we were talking, my doubts increased further. I had zero idea how to approach creating a YouTube channel or how the YouTube system even worked. On top of that, there already were big-time

YouTubers who produced this type of content.

After a lot of discussion, I decided that, even though I had no experience, I could learn and give it my all. If someday I had regrets about not succeeding with a YouTube channel, I could at least say that I gave it everything I had. I had always considered myself tech savvy, and I was up for the task. One of the things that convinced me was the possibility of passive income. Therefore, I decided to take the plunge and fully submerge myself.

Initially, I felt like a fish out of water. I had no idea what I was doing. Essentially, I had to learn what felt like an entirely new language. Every day, I had a million questions and no idea where to begin. Thankfully, I had a colleague who was already successful on YouTube and who provided me with essential knowledge when I felt stuck. As I began to plug away, day in and day out, I gradually climbed the learning curve through trial and error. I used Google searches, YouTube videos (how apt!), and other resources to increase my knowledge, and after a while, the process became seamless and simplified. I learned what worked and what did NOT work. As things became more clear, I kept up with my research and continued learning to fine-tune my methods. Thanks to that persistence, I can now confidently say that I have become fluent in the language of YouTube.

As the channel kept growing and we started to earn money on a consistent basis, I began to realize what a YouTube channel can do in terms of income and marketing power. Having a successful YouTube channel is like owning a store that is open 24 hours a day without the need for employees. Unlike a store, YouTube virtually has no overhead costs, which makes it a very low-risk endeavor financially. The only thing you cannot get back when pursuing a YouTube channel is the time you have invested. However, when you invest your time correctly, you start to generate organic views.

Once you reach that point, the process truly starts to become profitable and enjoyable. Even today, I find myself checking the numbers several times a day because our channel is growing on its own and we are accomplishing our goal of helping people that we can't see in the clinical setting. There is also a financial incentive to publish more videos, of course. Once you start generating income, it really becomes fun.

Since we began the channel, I have learned a lot of things that give our channel an advantage and that many people find helpful. There are definitely more successful channels than mine out there, but I know what I did to make mine work. If you would like to make this process easier for you and use our channel as a model, I encourage you to check it out and subscribe. That way, you can see what I am talking about in several examples. The name of the channel is *Physical Therapy 101*. We provide a slew of videos on ailments and how to treat them with physical therapy. Like I said, this book is a guide for beginners that want to embark on the YouTube journey. It is common to have doubts and even more common to feel like you might be wasting your time. Take it from me, if you follow the methods I lay out, you will allow your channel to grow organically just like I did. Also, before we begin, I want to offer you my email address in case you have questions regarding anything in your YouTube journey. I can be reached at nickgallodpt@gmail.com. I cannot promise that I will respond right away but I definitely will be available in case you need something answered.

The Benefits of YouTube

Starting a YouTube channel has several benefits that you may or may not know already. These benefits really speak for themselves, whether you want to use YouTube for business or for another purpose.

Benefit 1: Free Advertising

One of the best reasons to begin a YouTube channel is the free advertising. If you think about it, YouTube is not just a video website. It is a search engine. YouTube is currently the second largest search engine, behind only Google. Have you ever wanted to know something or how to do something, so you just YouTube'd it? I know I have! That is why YouTube is so incredibly popular. I have used it to look for video games, to fix things, to exercise, you name it. I have also seen businesses advertise their services on there. If you can get a video trending on YouTube, that is an excellent opportunity to drive more customers to your business.

Since YouTube is free, you can start a channel with zero overhead costs. That is a big bonus of social media marketing as a whole. If you think about all the business expenses that people have to endure to start a business, it can seem very intimidating. Some businesses require physical locations and equipment to operate. YouTube, on the other hand, requires no real estate, and your equipment costs to operate on a day-to-day basis are zero. Also, you need virtually zero employees to have your channel operational if you know what you are doing. Now, there are a few things that I would highly suggest spending money on because their implementation has helped us grow our channel. That doesn't mean they are 100% necessary, but I do recommend on. More on that later.

Benefit 2: YouTube Marketing Works on Google

"Google it" is a common phrase that we have become accustomed to. Google is the most popular search engine in the world. Did you know that YouTube is a subsidiary of Google? If you do a Google search for something, you may notice that recommended videos pop up. This happens because the two companies are intertwined, so people can access your content by simply doing a Google search. If a video from your channel shows up in the first three results, chances are people will click on it. We got lucky with our channel and had this happen in the initial stages of starting our channel. Right now, if you do a Google search for "Frozen Shoulder Pulleys," you will see that our Physical Therapy 101 video is the first result. Ranking high on YouTube and Google is the main reason why that video is so successful.

I want to share a quick story to illustrate this. A mutual friend of a colleague and me was sent to physical therapy for having frozen shoulder. At the clinic, they were given a set of pulleys and told to watch OUR video for home treatment. The amazing part is that this happened in an entirely different state and we are not affiliated with that medical practice! In other words, once you start trending on YouTube, you will pop up in people's general searches and those people will recommend your content to others.

Benefit 3: Your Content Is Always Searchable

Unless you are violating YouTube's terms or agreements when you make a video, it will be available forever. This means that once you publish the video, it is ALWAYS searchable. You will be able to find it in weeks, months, years. Other social media platforms require people to constantly keep up and publish new things to generate money. YouTube, on the other hand, allows your content to stay out there and generate income.

Benefit 4: Grow a Worldwide Audience

A massive advantage of having a YouTube channel is the fact that you can go worldwide with your content. For instance, you can periodically check where in the world your content is being viewed. I am a huge advocate for translating your titles and subtitles into all major languages, as it allows your videos to potentially trend in all areas of the world. Remember, the country that you are in is not the only place where people would like to see your content. I will discuss this in more detail further on.

Benefit 5: Audience Members Will Promote and Buy From You

As your audience grows and your content becomes more popular, your loyal audience members will actively participate in promoting your channel and even buying merchandise. You have probably noticed that people are constantly sharing videos on social media they think are funny or helpful. This is the type of audience you want to attract, which is easy to do on YouTube. YouTubers commonly post affiliate links in their video descriptions and have clickable icons on the videos themselves so that you can purchase products featured in the video. More information about this later.

How Do YouTubers Make Money?

—————

Now that you know why I am partial to having a YouTube channel, let's talk about the important part – how YouTubers generate money. YouTubers can generate income in several ways.

First off, once you reach specific requirements, you are in the so-called YouTube Partner Program, or the YPP for short. Once you qualify for this, you are allowed to include ads in your videos. That way, you can make money each time people watch one of your videos. If someone watching the video decides to click on that ad, it will generate even more money. That is why you see ads on nearly every video you watch these days. This is the first goal when developing a YouTube channel because it allows you to generate a very basic passive income every time a video is watched. I remember qualifying for this program like it was yesterday. It made me feel like I had truly made it in the world of YouTube!

YouTubers also make money through affiliate marketing. If you go to a popular YouTube video, there will probably be a link somewhere that takes you to something available for purchase. In affiliate marketing, you earn income every time you promote somebody else's products or services. Usually, the owner of the product or service pays an individual to advertise their products and services. A very popular example of this is Amazon affiliate marketing. I use this marketing program and have seen it generate some solid passive income. With this affiliate program, you provide links to products on Amazon that viewers can click on. I will elaborate on this in a later chapter.

There is another source of income, one that is usually reserved for the top YouTube channels – sponsorships. A sponsorship for YouTube works similarly to where a large company would sponsor something outside of YouTube. For example, if a YouTube channel has a sponsorship with a company such as Nike, you may see links or blurbs about Nike during their videos. I do not have experience with this aspect of YouTube yet, but I hope to change that in the future.

The YouTube Partner Program

Now that we know the basics of how YouTube channels make money, let's go into detail on the basic form of income, i.e. qualifying for ads. As I said before, this is known as the YouTube Partner Program (YPP). You are probably wondering, "What are the requirements for the YPP?" Good! From the start, your number one goal is to get into this program. The requirements CAN change; therefore, I highly encourage you to search the current requirements to make sure they are still consistent with what I am saying. Currently, the requirements are as follows:

- You must be in a country or region where the YPP is available. These countries are listed on YouTube's website.
- You need to meet the minimum threshold of 1,000 YouTube subscribers.
- You need to have 4,000 watch hours or more in the last 12 months.
- You need to have a linked AdSense account.

Once you have met these requirements, your channel will go into review, and based on that review, YouTube will either accept or decline you. If you feel discouraged after reading the list, I know the EXACT feeling. YouTube added these requirements right before we began our channel. I literally checked our channel every day and practically counted down the months, weeks, and days to when we would qualify for this program. I have heard of people who qualified in less than a year, but for others it takes longer. It took us a little over a year to finally qualify for the YPP.

1. YPP To-Do List

YouTube offers a great checklist for the YPP, and I highly encourage you to follow it. You can complete a lot of these steps prior to being accepted into the YPP. By doing that, you can save valuable time during the YouTube review process. First and foremost, you should make sure that your channel is in complete compliance with YouTube's terms and conditions. This includes all of their updated policies and guidelines. You do not want to go through all the hard work only to find out that you have been declined for major violations, so I highly encourage you to read the terms and conditions first.

The next item on the list is achieving 1,000 subscribers and 4,000 hours of watch time, which is the threshold YouTube requires for a channel to be eligible for the YPP. This is the item on the list where nearly everyone starts giving up because they are not seeing the type of growth they desire. But believe me, when you are ultimately accepted into the YPP, it is a massive achievement. I will go over strategies to help mitigate the difficulties you can face when trying to achieve this benchmark.

One thing that is important to do is sign the YPP terms. You can access these terms by going to your YouTube channel under "Creator Studio," and clicking

"Monetization." There won't be much in this section as long as you are under the threshold, but you can click "Notify me when I'm eligible." It means you will get a notification when you can finally submit the formal application.

Another item on the list is linking a Google AdSense account. This is easy and fairly quick to do. If you go to Google and type in, "Sign up for Google AdSense," you will be directed to the website where you can begin this process. It is important to note that if you have an existing Google AdSense account that has already been approved, then you can use that one to proceed. You can only link one Google AdSense account to the channel to meet this requirement, so pick one and stick with it.

The final item on the list is the YouTube review of your application. The review process happens once all prior items on the list have been fulfilled. The reason why I suggested to complete all prior items before going through the review process is that this review process can take several weeks to a month. The YouTube website states that you can expect the review "typically about 1 month after you meet the threshold." Therefore, having all your ducks in a row prior to this step can help save much valuable time, and it gives you a higher chance of approval.

There are two possible results after the review: you are accepted to the program, OR you are rejected. If you are accepted, then congratulations, you have reached the first tier of YouTube monetization! If you are rejected, do not be discouraged. You can apply again 30 days later to try to get accepted. People are usually rejected because their channel is not meeting the YouTube policies and guidelines. That is why it is imperative to know the terms and conditions before starting this entire process.

2. Going from 0 to 1,000 Subscribers

Maybe the subscriber threshold of 1,000 seems impossible to you; however, there are many ways to increase your number of subscribers. While 1,000 is the absolute magic number, the journey to this number can be a frustrating and stressful one. You probably won't reach this number of subscribers in one day, one week, one month, or even one year (although some people achieve this). The road from 0 to 1,000 subscribers to your channel is the period when you can experiment with the type of styles, content, and editing that people like on your channel. This is the most common time for people to give up on their YouTube journey and completely abandon their channel.

When you are just starting out with your channel, make sure you send the link to every family member, friend, acquaintance, etc. you can think of. They only need a Gmail account to subscribe to YouTube, and it is absolutely free. Likewise, it is free to hit that subscribe button for your channel. I began by sending my channel to several friends and family members and asked them to subscribe. I suggest that you ask people to subscribe to your channel only once you have several videos. I began to send out our channel after we had published 10 videos so that people had a good understanding of the type of content we were making. This also created opportunity, because people with certain injuries would subscribe and request future videos for treatment, thus giving us ideas. After getting started with a very small audience, we were able to gain some traction.

Another big thing in the beginning is constantly giving yourself exposure. It is important that, when you start to make a YouTube channel, you go all in with other social media sources as well. For example, *Physical Therapy 101* has a Facebook page, Twitter, Pinterest, and a website. Even though our presence on these other social media sources is not nearly as large, they all play a major role in something known as Search Engine Optimization, or SEO for short. This acronym is thrown around a lot regarding anything online. Essentially, it is the process of optimizing your website/social media in order to get organic unpaid views. Remember, Google and YouTube work hand in hand, so if you have great searchability on Google, this can translate to more views for your YouTube channel.

As we started to create more videos, I began to scour groups on social media for certain diagnoses and offer our channel as guidance. For example, we have that very successful video on frozen shoulder, so I joined several frozen shoulder support groups. Whenever someone had a question on treatment, I would post our video so that they could use it as a guide. I suggest searching any Facebook groups that are related to your content. Be sure to read the terms and conditions because there are instances when people will not appreciate people offering their videos.

Another great resource I used was Twitter. I created a separate Twitter account for Physical Therapy 101, and each time we launched a new video, I would post it on

Twitter with the appropriate hashtags. I then began to actively search for people posting about their ailments. People on Twitter are constantly posting things regarding their pains and diagnoses. Using frozen shoulder as an example, I would search for posts where people talked about their battles with frozen shoulder. They often asked for specific remedies for this condition. This was where I would reply with a post containing the link to our YouTube video. Most people were very appreciative for receiving this information, which allowed our video to get more attention.

Another great method I used to gain subscribers initially was looking at other physical therapy-related channels. People are constantly posting comments to videos with their feedback. I specifically looked for the ones that gave a video negative feedback. You can use these comments to your advantage! For example, if someone posts something like, "Good video but I can't hear you!" then you can comment saying, "Hey, we also have a video for this, hope it helps!" Believe it or not, but people are extremely receptive and responsive if you are willing to engage with their comments and respond to their concerns. Even if you do not have a video already filmed for a specific subject, this can give you an idea of what the audience is looking for on YouTube and can help you gain additional exposure.

3. *Things I Would Not Suggest to Gain Subscribers*

Once you start the YouTube channel journey, you will see ads saying that you can "pay for subscribers," and other services requiring money. There are several reasons why I highly suggest that you do not go this route. First and foremost, YouTube has been getting a lot better at tracking these types of services over the years and will not hesitate to ban channels that are using them. I have read that a lot of these services use bots and other means to help provide people with subscribers. YouTube has become very good at detecting fake accounts and subscribers and will eliminate them. Remember, YouTube will take your channel through a review process. If they discover you are buying subscribers during the review process, they will most likely fail you for it. If you are not banned for using this service, it is important to know that YouTube is always auditing channels. During this process, they delete subscribers from channels if they believe they are fake. For example, if you pay for 1,000 subscribers and only 90 are real, it is possible that your channel can drop from 1,000 to 90 after this auditing process.

In the rare instance that your channel has not been dinged for using this service and your subscriber number remains, remember you still have to meet the 4,000 watch hours to qualify for the YPP application. Therefore, if you have all those subscribers and hardly any views, you still need to do a lot of leg work to achieve the views. Therefore, it is best to achieve subscribers the right way. Building an audience that actually watches your channel pays out in the long run.

Another thing that some channels use to "boost" their subscribers is something known as "Follow for Follow." This is a method of gaining subscribers by subscribing to another channel and asking for them to subscribe back. I have never used this method, and I don't recommend it for several reasons. The first reason is that, most of the time, the other person does not follow you, so it's a waste of your time. But the main reason is that this tactic won't help you reach the view threshold. These people have usually subscribed to so many channels that they will never even see your videos be posted. Therefore, they will most likely never give you any views.

4. *Watch Time*

First, let's define "watch time." As you have probably guessed, it is the total amount of time that your audience spends watching your videos. In order to qualify for the YouTube Partner Program, a channel has to meet the minimum of 4,000 hours or 240,000 minutes within a 12-month timeframe. In the beginning, this number sounds impossible. We reached 1,000 subscribers quicker than we did the 4,000 total hours of watch time. However, it is important to remember that the more videos you have, the quicker you should progress to this milestone. There are also some key strategies that are very helpful.

It is important to know how YouTube measures watch time. YouTube calculates how much watch time your channel has in the last 365 days. In other words, your channel will need 4,000 hours of watch time in the prior 12 months. For example, if you pick a random date such as January 1, 2020, YouTube will calculate the 12-month total watch time by measuring all the way back to January 2, 2019. One thing to note is that if you happen to publish a very successful video or series of videos, you can achieve these 4,000 hours of watch time before the 12-month mark. For example, if you reach this threshold in three months and have met the subscriber mark, you are already eligible to apply for the YPP.

The best way to monitor watch time for your channel is logging into your channel and going to "Channel Analytics." Here, you can see the number of views, the amount of watch time, and the number of subscribers you have received in a recent span of time. The default is usually set for "last 28 days." Remember, you want to see how much watch time you have received in the last 365 days. In order to do this, you can select the "last 28 days" tab and change it to "last 365 days." This will give you the most accurate up-to-date watch time you have during this span of time. Also, be sure that you have "watch time" selected and not "views." Those are two common mistakes. If you avoid them, you can get an accurate estimate of where you are currently for watch time. Finally, if you want to get specific, you can click on specific days and see how much watch time you are receiving per day. You can take your average per day and extrapolate it to 365 days to see if you will hit the 4,000 hours of watch time before the deadline. Remember though, the more videos you publish, the more your watch time will increase, so your current average will most likely increase as you publish more videos!

5. 4,000 Hours of Watch Time Strategies

There are several strategies out there about how to get the 4,000 hours of watch time. I used a particularly good exercise to achieve this landmark that I'd like to share with you. Let's break down the watch time figure into minutes: 4,000 hours of watch time computes to 240,000 minutes. YouTube prefers videos that are around 10 minutes long, so let's use that as a baseline. Here are a few options that can help you achieve this milestone:

1. You can make 240,000 videos of 10 minutes that each get 1 view.
2. You can make 2,400 videos of 10 minutes that each get 10 views.
3. You can make 240 videos of 10 minutes that each get 100 views.

Out of these three scenarios, number three is the most likely one to attain. If you break down this scenario, it means that you need to publish a video every 1.5 days within a 365-day time frame. Remember, this is just a baseline, but it is important to maintain a schedule of weekly content to attract new viewers. Now, this DOES NOT mean that you absolutely need to create 240 videos before you are able to achieve the YPP. It just means that you should aim for this number, but as you begin to create content that becomes increasingly popular, you can achieve the necessary watch time way before the 240-videos mark. I will discuss this in more detail later, but if you notice that a video is starting to take off compared to the rest, try to produce more of that content. Remember to always give your viewers what they want. The numbers will always indicate what is most popular. Also, just because a video does not initially get a lot of exposure, that does not necessarily mean it will never become popular. Videos are constantly becoming increasingly popular due to the YouTube algorithm.

We got closer to the YPP around 100 videos or so, but that had to do with our content being discovered and watched as it gained popularity. Also, the search volume for the topics we were highlighting increased. If you can crack into a topic that gets a lot of views and that people are actively searching for, then I highly suggest to make more of those videos. Take your most popular videos and keep publishing content associated with it. People often start making other content and completely ignore what is working, which is WRONG. Keep going with the content that works and give your audience what they want!

6. *Things I would Not Suggest to Gain Watch Time*

Just like for subscribers, there are services that boost your watch time. Once again, I have never used any type of service like this, and I do not recommend it because you do not want to compromise your good standing with YouTube. From what I understand, there are several types of view services out there, ranging from non-human views to human views, and a "view for view" strategy. The bottom line is, using any type of service that fraudulently boosts your views for your YouTube channel is frowned upon. This can end with YouTube banning you from the platform. Also, these services are usually not free and can apparently become very time-consuming. If people enjoy the videos you are publishing, then you will NEVER have to use these services and things will progress organically.

YouTube Terms

Now that you know the process to get into the YPP and some strategies that can be implemented to get there, it is important that you know two widely used YouTube terms. These terms are not very complicated, but if you do not know what they refer to, it can be confusing.

1.   Cost Per Mille (CPM)

Once you are accepted into the program, you will see the acronym CPM thrown around a lot when it comes to generating revenue. CPM literally means "cost per mille." Mille is Latin for "thousand." On YouTube, the CPM is the cost per 1,000 views. In other words, it is the money an advertiser pays each time their advertisement is watched 1,000 times. What is important to realize is that not all of the money of the CPM goes directly to the creator. YouTube takes a cut, but that does not mean it is not worth it. There are several other ways to generate money; ads are just one of them. You can access CPM by going to your channel and clicking on "Channel Analytics," and then going to "Revenue." If you are not currently in the YPP, your Revenue section will not be displayed.

2.   Revenue Per Mille (RPM)

RPM is defined as "Revenue per Mille." This is essentially how much the creator is being paid per 1,000 views. It is calculated after YouTube has taken their cut out of the ad revenue and gives a fairly accurate representation of how much you will receive. You can access it in the same place on your channel. Click on "Channel Analytics," and then go to "Revenue." Just like CPM, if you are currently not in the YPP, the revenue section will be unavailable until you qualify.

Planning Before Filming

Now that you have a great understanding of the YPP and some strategies that I used to get there, let's talk about filming. I want to discuss key strategies I implemented that I believe have led to my channel's success. These strategies can really help you save time, and potentially money, because there are a lot of things you can purchase that claim to help you. I do not want you to waste your time and money with any of these gimmicks, so I have only included things that worked for me.

1. Pick Your Industry

This probably goes without saying, but it is important to choose an industry that you enjoy and that you are knowledgeable and passionate about. If you look at most successful channels, the creators are engaging and knowledgeable on their subjects, but they also really enjoy it. This not only makes you appear more competent, but it will also make it a much more enjoyable experience for you. Personally, I am passionate about physical therapy because I enjoy helping people and I do this day in and day out. I have learned things in school and during my clinical experiences that can help a lot of people. I have found that even the simplest things that I do day in and day out can help a wide range of people when it is in video format. Therefore, think about things that you do frequently. These tasks may seem monotonous for you, but odds are that people are out there searching for how to do it on their own.

Another thing to consider is how a YouTube channel can benefit your everyday life. In the field of physical therapy, I am not only meeting new people every day, but I am also repeating a lot of what I say over and over. On top of that, a major part of physical therapy is assigning home exercise programs. Typically, a client is given a piece of paper showing the exercises, which I have always thought might be confusing. People also lose the piece of paper eventually, BUT they usually have their cell phone on them. Therefore, once we began talking about beginning a YouTube channel, I knew that it would make my life easier and be more beneficial to my patients. If incorporating a YouTube channel can improve your daily life, then I highly encourage it. Regardless of your industry, there are most likely tasks and things that you are repeating over and over, day in and day out. Think about filming those and what others would like to learn. Sometimes the simplest tasks at your job can get the most views!

A YouTube channel is also a great marketing tool when used correctly. Remember, YouTube is a subsidiary of Google, which is used by millions of people every single day. Certain search terms yield YouTube videos as their results, and if you can appear in these search results, then your views and popularity will skyrocket. In the early days of my channel, we had a video start to get a ton of views each day, and I was curious as to why this was happening. I Googled two words associated with the topic, and sure enough, our video came up as the first result.

The same thing can be said about many other industries. If you are constantly meeting new people like I am, then you should absolutely create a YouTube channel. These are customers that you are meeting in real life, and if they are pleased with you, they will subscribe and tell people about your videos. The awesome thing about the social media age is that, as you build these customers, they will be more inclined to share your videos with others.

If you look on YouTube, there are various industries that people have made channels of which get a ton of attention and views. People love to look up things they can do themselves, whether it is fixing something or creating something.

2. Find a Mentor

Like I mentioned before, my journey began with someone that had experience in this field. I absolutely suggest that everyone begins there. As the saying goes, "Don't reinvent the wheel." This was a very helpful step for me because whenever I had questions regarding the channel, my mentor could answer them for me. In the beginning, you will have a lot of questions. If you have access to someone who has already been through the process, they will know the ins and the outs of this entire process.

If you do not have access to a mentor, not all hope is lost. There were several times when I did not want to bother my mentor or I felt like the answer was easy for me to find on my own. Pretty much all the information you need is already on the internet. You can pay for webinars (which I did not do). I know people who have gone this route and who told me it was beneficial for them. If you do not want to pay for webinars, you can find a lot of the information for free; you just need to know where to look.

Moreover, I suggest finding a friend who also wants to start a YouTube channel. It makes things easier because you can each bounce ideas off of each other and you can talk about your personal experiences with each other. For instance, I know someone who has a YouTube channel about real estate. He has been doing it longer than I have, but we each have unique ideas that we frequently talk to each other about. Why repeat the trial and error that someone else has done when you can find out what works by simply talking to them? Knowing someone else with a YouTube channel will also give you opportunities to make collaboration videos and increase your exposure.

3. Look at the Industry Leaders

One thing of vast importance is to find the leaders in your industry. It's important to see what the current leaders in your niche are doing and how they are designing their channel. This helps immensely regarding channel development, because you may not know where to start. Finding the current leader in your niche will show you what has been working and what has not. I began this process by going to the search bar and typing in "Physical Therapy." For instance, if you are interested in photography or another topic, type that in the search bar. I also wanted to look directly at channels, so I filtered the search results to only display channels.

After I had the search results I wanted, I followed the

top three channels with the most subscribers because I knew they got a lot of exposure. I started to scour their channels and made a list of topics that got the most views and things that did not do so well. After this, I watched videos in each channel and got a feel for how they were designing their videos. I took note of things I liked and did not like. This is an important step because it is how you help yourself be different than everybody else. It is also extremely beneficial because you can model your channel in a similar format, or you can choose to go a completely different route.

Finding successful industry leaders also showed me that the subject matter we wanted to publish was in high demand. This is reassuring because sometimes there is great content on YouTube, but it is just not in great demand. This does not mean that it will never be in demand, but certain topics are just not searched very much. Now, I am not telling you to not create a channel because nobody has ever done it. I have read plenty of success stories of people who are the first in their niche. What I am saying, however, is that if there already is great demand for a certain topic, then this may increase the chances of its success.

4. *Use the Comments Section*

You can learn even more from the leading channels by diving into the comments section of their videos. I think the importance of this section on YouTube is often overlooked. The comments section is filled with a slew of information that is very valuable. For instance, you will see people commenting what they like and what they do not like. This is where you can start to separate yourself from the competition. Go to one of the industry leaders that you are modeling and scan their comments section. You may see people that are pleased with what they are doing, but you may also see viewers that are less impressed. "Can you do a video for so and so?" This is a common thing you will see, and it is a good opportunity for you to try and gain subscribers.

When we first started our channel, I saw a comment on another channel asking for a video on ankle tendinitis. We decided to film a video treating this very condition. When the video was completed, I went back to this comment and posted our video as a reply. This person thanked me and then subscribed to our channel. I realize this is tedious, but subscribers are extremely important in the initial phase. Therefore, you want to do everything you can to gain subscribers each day. Hopefully, after people subscribe to your channel, they will share new videos that you publish with friends and family, thus helping you to increase your exposure.

This is also beneficial if you have a lot of videos already, because you can comment and post the link to what people are requesting. However, make sure NOT TO SPAM someone's channel. You don't want them to report you for spamming their channel and have YouTube take action against you. Commenting on one or two comments should not cause any trouble. This is extremely effective because you are talking to people that are prone to subscribe to channels, and you are making them aware that you like to engage with the commenters. With this approach you are giving people what they want, and they will be more inclined to subscribe to your channel and watch your videos. You are also showing potential subscribers that you listen to the audience and engage with them, which is rare amongst YouTube content creators.

5. Determine What Is in Demand

It can be extremely hard to determine what is in demand, but once you develop your own formula, it becomes A LOT easier. Initially, we were making videos that we thought would be most helpful, but there are ways to determine which videos are in demand. Think of a topic that you are interested in and then do a YouTube search. Does the video currently exist? If not, then make it! If it does exist, how many videos are there and how do they look? Chances are there are videos for the content already, but people love to see improved videos. I can't tell you how many times I have designed videos based on popular ones that were either not very clear or had poor audio.

A great way to determine what people are searching for is typing things into the YouTube search bar without hitting "enter." We have all most likely seen this by now, but as you begin to type in YouTube, the search bar begins to suggest search items for you. For example, if I am thinking about doing a video for lower back stretches, I will go to YouTube and type in the word "lower." As soon as this word is in the search bar, I am presented with a slew of possibilities that a lot of people search for. This can give you an indication of the content people are interested in.

Begin Filming

When you have a good feel for your niche and the leaders in the industry, you should begin the filming process. You want to use the data you have collected so far to determine how to film properly. For example, in our videos, we demonstrate certain exercises or show specific diagnoses. We decided to do this because we did not want to film ourselves giving a long speech. In our experience, people gave negative feedback on that type of content. Therefore, all of our videos are short, sweet, and to the point. Not all industries are like this, but that is why it's important to collect as many data as possible beforehand. That way you do not waste any time filming videos people do not like.

You also want to make sure that you choose an appropriate space to film in. Typically, people film in their offices, bedrooms, and other areas in a building. Some people film outside during events. Whatever location you choose, make sure that the background and area where you are filming are not distracting from your content.

This probably goes without saying, but you should maintain great quality for your videos. People do not want to see bad-quality videos with poor visuals and bad audio. They want to see videos that are clear, to the point, and easy to understand. For our *Physical Therapy 101* channel, we shoot every video with a 4k camera.

One element that I recommend you include for your videos is a quick few words telling your viewers to subscribe to your channel. We add this to most of our videos; if you watch one, you will hear our request to subscribe towards the end. You can add a quick blurb at the beginning or the end which may entice the viewer to subscribe. You can also ask the viewer to "hit the thumbs up button" if they like the video to help you gain some exposure.

Necessary Equipment

Now I would like to discuss the necessary equipment to start a YouTube channel. These are the items that I started with, and I still use a lot of them. There are a lot of options out there, so you should choose what feels like the best fit. If you are anything like me, you want to minimize your expenses upfront, which is perfectly possible. Therefore, I want to give you a list of items you can use right away without breaking the bank.

1. Camera

This is the most obvious piece of equipment that you need to start a YouTube channel. A camera is absolutely essential. There are thousands of cameras out there, and everyone uses a different one, but I want to assure you that it is not necessary to buy the most expensive camera right off the bat. For starting out, I would recommend something simple such as a webcam or a camcorder, as long as it records clearly in 1080p. You want your audience to be able to see you and be drawn to what you are trying to show them. If you have issues with visibility, it will be very difficult for people to stay drawn to watching your videos.

A great option for beginners is to simply use your cellphone. Believe it or not, a lot of popular YouTubers started out that way! If you go the cellphone route, be sure to run a few test videos and verify that everything appears nicely when you upload the videos to YouTube. One essential thing: I highly recommend to film horizontally with your cellphone. Filming this way is superior to filming vertically, because when you upload to YouTube, it will fill the entire screen as opposed to part of the screen.

2. *External Microphone*

Regardless of what type of camera you use to record your videos, it is very important that your audience hears you clearly. I have seen several videos online that were filmed exceptionally well, but the audience was not receptive to the content because it was extremely difficult to hear. To prevent this, it is crucial to have an external microphone so that your audio compliments your video. I don't have any specific recommendation for the type of microphone, as long as it is something that allows you to be heard clearly in your videos. Just make sure that the type of microphone you choose is compatible with your camera.

3. *Tripod*

This is something a lot of successful YouTubers use, and I highly recommend it. A tripod allows you to record yourself steadily without any camera shaking so that your audience can stay fully engaged. If you have ever watched videos with a lot of shakiness, you know it can almost give you a headache! Therefore, I suggest investing in a tripod for the camera you decide on. Please note that the type of tripod you need depends on the type of content you are filming. If you have an active channel where you are always moving, there are items out there that can help you stabilize your shot while you're on the go.

4. Lighting

Another important feature that helps attract people is the amount of lighting in your videos. Lighting equipment is definitely necessary if you are filming indoors and in dimly lit areas. Even if you are filming in areas with adequate lighting, additional well-placed lights can help even out the brightness in the environment.

5. Video Editing Software

If you are doing the video edits yourself, then you absolutely need video editing software. There are many types of software out there. I have experience with iMovie. If you have a Mac, chances are you already have iMovie experience. If not you, can install it for free and play around with it. It is extremely easy to use, and there are many tutorials out there that can make you proficient in it in no time. If you have a PC, it is not yet possible to run iMovie. Therefore, the best course of action is to check out what software is available and what cost you are comfortable with.

Upload to YouTube as Private

Now that the editing process is complete, upload the video to your channel, but do NOT make it public yet. It is important that you keep it private until you have systematically chosen all the proper elements that will help make your video get maximum exposure. Make sure your video contains all of these necessary elements that help your audience find the video.

Video Elements –
Definitions and Examples

———

Once you upload a video to private, there are a few essential things. These are the necessary elements that you are required to input before you publish the video for the public to see. Some of these things are absolutely required, and others are highly suggested in my opinion. The point is to help your video gain more exposure. If you can do this process effectively, then your videos will gain exposure over time, your watch time and number of subscribers can dramatically increase, and you can apply for the YPP quicker. I follow these exact steps when launching a new video.

1. Title

The first basic piece of information that your video needs is a great title. The thing to keep in mind when designing a title is how search friendly it is.

Tips: Think of how someone who is new to the topic would search for it. For example, if you want to do a video on publishing a book, imagine how users would search for it. Most likely, they would search something like "How to write a book" or "Publishing a book," things of that nature. A great way to determine the searchability of a title is to go directly to the YouTube search bar. You will probably notice that, as you begin to type something in the search bar, word suggestions show up below. These are ranked in descending order of popularity of searches on YouTube. Play around and see which title flows best while putting your title in the search bar to get the most optimized title possible.

Example: Go to my YouTube channel and find the video titled "Frozen Shoulder Physical Therapy Pulley Exercises." When people are diagnosed with this condition, they are usually assigned a pulley and told they have "Frozen Shoulder." The medical diagnosis is "Adhesive Capsuilitis," but I know that most diagnosed people will not be searching for those words. They are often assigned to physical therapy and given exercises, hence why our video has this title.

2. Description

The description is located beneath each video and provides details about the video to potential viewers. When descriptions are written well, they can help users find videos.

Many things can go into an effective description. First and foremost, you should try and determine one or two keywords that are essential to your video. Include those keywords throughout the description. For example, if we go back to our example regarding publishing a book, maybe a keyword that you would like to include a lot is the word "publish." This word should be used several times in the description (I usually shoot for two or three times). Whatever keyword you decide on, it is important that this keyword is also in your title for optimal searchability.

Another important part of writing a description is

using complimentary keywords. What I mean by this is that you use keywords that show relation to each other. If your first keyword is, "publish," then your next keyword should be something related, such as "book." Having related keywords helps you rank better for Google and YouTube searches.

It is ALWAYS a good idea to tell people what to expect. You do not want to misrepresent your video, because maybe people will become frustrated and click through it without watching. Therefore, it is important to be truthful with your audience on what to expect when watching your video. Remember to always try to "write like a human." Make sure you use language your audience understands. They may not understand fully what you are discussing unless you explain it in simple terms.

Use your keywords in the first few sentences of your description. This is known as "front loading," which is important for several reasons. First and foremost, the YouTube algorithm prioritizes the first few sentences of your description for SEO. This is where you should include your keywords. It is also important to include keywords in the beginning because when people search for videos, the first few sentences appear directly below the title.

Once you have described your video effectively and in a way that people can understand, chances are they will want to see more about your video. This is why it is important to include a few links in the video description so you can promote your brand more.

Example: Go to my YouTube channel and find the

video titled, "L5 S1 Disc Bulge Exercises - Lumbar Radiculopathy Treatment." This video gained a lot of momentum fairly fast, due to several factors including the optimization of the description. If you look at the description, you will see the first line includes an affiliate link to a product featured in the video. That way, the viewer can easily purchase it if they want to. Then the video is described in a way the viewer can understand. After doing some research, I determined that L5 S1, disc bulge, and radiculopathy receive a lot of searches because it is a common diagnosis among people with lower back pain. Therefore, these terms are included in the title and description. After the details of the video, viewers can see more of the description where I provide a link to our website so they can find more information.

3. Thumbnail

The thumbnail for a video is the image that a viewer sees before they click on the video. It is the first impression people get prior to clicking, so it is essential that the thumbnail looks appealing. YouTube gives you a default thumbnail for each video you upload, but I don't recommend using these because custom thumbnails lead to better results.

First and foremost, there are some size requirements so that the thumbnail appears properly. Here are the thumbnail size requirements taken directly from the YouTube support website:

- Have a resolution of 1280x720 (with a minimum width of 640 pixels).

- Be uploaded in image formats such as JPG, GIF, or PNG.
- Remain under the 2MB limit.
- Try to use a 16:9 aspect ratio as it's the most used in YouTube players and previews.

Following the basic size requirements is important so that the image appears properly to the viewer. Be sure to confirm these size requirements because they may change depending on the updates on YouTube.

The next essential tip for thumbnail design is to use a great image as the thumbnail background. This can be a separate image or a clip from the video that you are uploading. Typically, I use an image from the video that we are uploading, but either option works as long as it is a strong visual that attracts attention. I have seen people have success with stock images, custom images from other sources, and even images they have purchased.

Another thing I like to do when designing my thumbnails is include text in the image. An image may grab a viewer's attention, but reading additional information about the video is more likely to get them to click. In order to make the thumbnail more appealing, I include a few keywords in the title so that the thumbnail is as descriptive as possible. Avoid using any clickbait text that misleads your audience, because then they will be reluctant to watch the entire thing. Also, be sure to choose a very clear font so that the text is readable. Feel free to check my channel's thumbnails for ideas. It would also be worth your while to check the thumbnails of the videos of channels in your industry to get a feel for what works.

Example: Go to my YouTube channel and find the video titled, "L5 Disc Bulge Exercises - Lumbar Radiculopathy Treatment." In this video's thumbnail, you will see someone demonstrating the exercise, an anatomical image representing L5 Radiculopathy, and the text "Back Pain Relief!" The thumbnail has visual appeal. In addition, most people dealing with this type of injury are usually affected by back pain, so that's why I've added that specific text.

4. *Playlists*

A playlist is a collection of videos.

Playlists are a great tool when it comes to uploading YouTube videos. You can create a collection of related videos that can be grouped together. For example, on our channel, we have playlists generated for specific body parts/injuries such as the lower back.

Add every video that you film to a playlist. These playlists are very useful for viewers because related content is grouped together. Playlists keep viewers engaged and allow them to search for more videos on your channel with similar content.

Example: We have several playlists on YouTube, so you can see how we grouped them appropriately. Be sure to also check how the leaders in your industry are creating their playlists so you can see exactly how it is working for someone currently doing it.

5.   Cards

Cards are notifications that can pop up during the video in order for you to promote numerous things, such as your brand and/or other videos on your channel.

Place at least one card per video. Cards show the viewer that you have more content related to what they are currently viewing, which may create additional views on your other videos. You have probably seen a video where someone is talking about a specific topic and something flashes on the screen linking to another one of their videos. This is the effective way to use cards. Make sure you do not use cards excessively throughout the video because that may cause the viewer to leave. Remember, if the video is designed like one that you would watch, other people will watch it as well.

Example: Go to my YouTube channel and find the video, "SI Joint Pain - Stretches for Pain Relief." When the video reaches the 31-second mark, you will see a card pop up at the top of the screen that begins with, "Suggested: L5 S1 Disc Bulge Exercises - Lumbar Radiculopathy Tre…" If the viewer clicks on it, it takes them straight to that video. This card was added specifically because people with SI Joint Pain can also have another condition such as an L5 S1 disc bulge. The card is my attempt to keep people's attention and hopefully direct them to another helpful video.

6. End Screens

End screens are the end of a video, where you can include multiple elements, such as links to other videos, links to other playlists, links to other channels, links to subscribe to your channel, and links to promote other things, such as your website.

At the end of every single video I publish, I place a link to subscribe to the channel as well as another link to the playlist the video belongs to. Remember, the goal is to always point your viewers to other material that you have published online or are trying to promote. By giving viewers this opportunity at the end of the video, you are increasing your chances of them clicking on more of your links.

Example: Go to the video on my channel titled, "6 Calf Strengthening Exercises." This video is one of our most watched videos, and we have had great success with the content. If you go to the end of the video, at the time mark of 1:14, a link to subscribe to our channel and a link to the rest of the playlist pop up. This is our attempt to get the viewer to watch more of our content and to earn their subscription.

7. Tags

Tags are defined as descriptive keywords that can be added to the published video so viewers can find your content. In order to find great tags, take a look at how you were able to determine your title based on using the search bar.

8. Translate Into Different Languages

I actually began translating all my videos into different languages by accident. At work, I treat people that are non-English speakers and who prefer their native language. One day, a client came in with lower back pain, and they only spoke Spanish. I was about to give them the link to a video, but it was only in English and I did not want to confuse them. I knew there was a way to translate your video into different languages, but I was not sure how. After doing a lot of research, I figured out how to translate this one video and add a Spanish title, description, and subtitles so that they could follow along.

In the beginning, I had no idea how to translate the dialogue in our videos. But the neat thing about YouTube is that you have the capability to provide numerous translations for each video you upload. It is completely up to you which languages you add, but I started by doing the languages that my current clients preferred. I do this by translating literally every piece of information about the video: I translate the title, description, and then provide a corresponding subtitle. Believe it or not, people will use these translations, and if your channel goes viral in a certain country, it can result in a huge amount of views, watch time, and exposure. For example, we have some videos that are extremely popular in other countries and not as popular in others. If we had limited our channel to English, we would never have known its maximum potential.

Translating in different languages not only helped my

current clients at work, but it also helped our exposure! This was another way to separate myself from the competition because I noticed that many of the major channels were only available in English. Then, as my channel began to generate views, I looked at our demographics to see where we were getting views specifically. For example, initially I was not translating our videos into Filipino because we were not generating views there. Over time, however, I began to notice a small percentage of views coming from the Philippines, so I started to including the language in my translation process.

It is important that you translate the following elements: title, description, and subtitles. This not only allows people to search for the video in their native language, but they can also follow along and read what you are talking about in their native language. Over time, your videos will begin to accumulate views from other areas. A major thing to be cautious of is to make sure all the words in the English subtitles are spelled correctly! When you begin to translate subtitles, YouTube will use the original language to translate from. If words are misspelled, the translation will not happen correctly. I always give the English subtitles a look-over before I begin the translation process.

Examples: Go to my YouTube channel and find the video titled, "How to Release the Psoas Muscle - Pso Rite Muscle Release." This video is not only getting views in the United States but also in the rest of the world. If you click the "subtitles" button and then click "settings," you can see all the languages that are available for the video. As the audio moves on in English, the text will follow in the language selected. Also, if you like, you can set the native language for your YouTube account to one of those languages listed, and the video title and description will also come up in that language.

After the Video Is Launched Publicly

Once you have done all of the above and you are happy with the finished product, it is time to launch the video for the public! When you have reached this step, I recommend following a few more steps to make sure that your video gains maximum exposure. If you do this correctly, your video will be able to gain steady views and help your channel to grow organically.

1.   Give Your Video a Thumbs Up!

The number of thumbs up can influence the YouTube algorithm in a positive or negative manner. Therefore, since you already have an account, it's only logical to give your video its first thumbs up. Now, you can do this several times if you have multiple YouTube accounts, but be careful; sometimes YouTube will do a check and recognize that you spammed likes. Therefore, it's best to just do one in the beginning.

Once you have given your video a thumbs up, send it out to your close personal friends and have them watch and give a thumbs up too. You will not have to keep doing this once you have reached the YPP, but this is absolutely helpful in the beginning. I did this for every video we launched at first, and it helped us grow rapidly.

2. Respond to Every Commenter

Initially, you want to get as much exposure as possible. People REALLY appreciate it if they get responses, and they typically get annoyed if they never get a response from the content creator. That is why I encourage you to respond to everyone who comments on your videos. It will help you build rapport with people and gain loyal followers. Anytime someone comments on one of my videos, I usually respond with, "Thank you for watching, hope the video was helpful for you!" This not only shows your appreciation, but also that you are very active on the platform.

The first time a person responds in a different language can be exciting and make you nervous. I know I experienced both! This is a unique opportunity to have subscribers and exposures in a different country so I highly suggest responding to those comments. I typically translate their comment using Google Translator and then comment back translating my dialogue into their language. I typically say something along the lines of, "Thank you for the feedback, hope the video is helpful." People really do appreciate it when you communicate back with them, and they will be more inclined to share your videos with people they know if you do this.

3. Share Videos on Many Social Media Platforms

If you want to have a successful YouTube channel, you need to use many other platforms to get maximum exposure. Using my channel as an example, we not only have a YouTube channel, but we also have accounts on Facebook, Twitter, Instagram, Patreon, Blogger, and Pinterest. Each one of these accounts refers to our website and YouTube channel. The YouTube channel ALSO refers to all of these social media platforms. You want to make sure that each account refers to the channel and ideally to your website. This allows your website and channel to appear in more links and increases the potential for exposure. Each time I launch a video, the video is shared on nearly all of these platforms to maximize its exposure

4. *Build a Website*

It is very important to start building your brand if you want to have a successful YouTube channel. A major way to do this is getting a website, which improves your search engine optimization (SEO). Make sure that your website refers to your channel and all other social media, and that your channel and social media refer to your website. For our channel, there is a corresponding web page with a slew of information on it for each diagnosis we feature. On the website you can provide additional information for the topic to help your brand grow. The website is also a huge resource if you add affiliate marketing (which I highly suggest).

5. *Use Affiliate Marketing*

A huge thing to incorporate into your YouTube channel is affiliate marketing. Affiliate marketing means that you get paid to promote another person's or company's product. I knew very little about this when I started out, but it is not as difficult as you may think. We currently do this through Amazon Affiliates, and it works like this: you put up a personalized link for a product or search, which a prospective buyer can click to make a purchase. Amazon will then give you a percentage based on this purchase. What is interesting about Amazon Affiliates is, if someone clicks your link but buys another item, you still get a percentage of that total purchase. You can find out more specifics if you search for "Amazon Affiliates," but I want to tell you how we use it to our advantage. In our videos, we sometimes use a product that helps in a recovery process. Commonly, we get asked where people can buy this product. In today's day and age, Amazon has a huge following, so this is a good way to generate additional income. The great thing is that it is predominantly passive.

One thing I want to talk about here is that we use a very subtle process when we are listing out affiliate products. I have learned that people do not really like the salesman approach when they are looking for things on YouTube. They want to know how to accomplish what they have inquired about, and they prefer to have the option to buy or not. If you are trying to sell something right off the bat, this can lead to negative comments.

Bonus Chapter:
Sign Up for Amazon Affiliates!

One thing that really helps maximize the amount of money you can make on YouTube is being in the Amazon Affiliates Program. Basically, this program allows you to make up to 10% of advertising fees with Amazon directly. This is accomplished via an Amazon Affiliate link that you can place on websites, in video descriptions, or anywhere on the internet. As long as someone clicks the link and buys the product, you get credit for it. Initially, it will seem extremely difficult to get any type of sales because you have not built a self-sustaining social media presence yet. Once this presence has been built, however, your audience will be more inclined to click on the links that you have used.

1. Reasons to Have an Amazon Affiliates Account

There are several reasons why it is useful to have an affiliation with Amazon. First and foremost, the most obvious benefit and the main reason why everyone uses it is that it can help you maximize your income. Once you reach the YPP, you already get paid each time the video is watched, so it only makes sense to try and make more money from the same video. Therefore, if you are featuring a product in the video or want to advertise any particular item available on Amazon, it is highly beneficial to provide an affiliate link for that so you get additional money.

Another good reason to have an Amazon Affiliate Account is that nearly everyone out there has some form of an Amazon account and trusts the platform. Therefore, if you post a link for a product you are featuring in a video or elsewhere and people click it, the process is streamlined and they are more inclined to purchase this item. Combined with Amazon's wide selection of goods and fast delivery, people will be more inclined to purchase something from an Amazon link.

Amazon also allows people to publish books in a specific program called Kindle Direct Publishing (KDP) for short. This is the exact process I used to publish this book. If you ever decide to venture into publishing your own products, then you can also advertise them with an affiliate link. If you think about it, that means you are making money from the profitable sale AND from your affiliate link.

Finally, Amazon is always growing. They continue to venture into other types of businesses and will continue to do so in the future. Therefore, if you are already an Amazon Affiliate, this will open you up for additional avenues as Amazon acquires other types of business interests.

2. *Using Amazon Affiliate Effectively*

One thing that we do for each video is provide an Amazon Affiliate link to a product or item that is either featured in or related to our video. I highly suggest you do the same thing for the reasons I listed above. It is extremely easy to do once you have signed up for an account. If you go to our videos, you will see that we feature the following line in the description: "Buy on Amazon: (example hyperlink)." This makes the link to the product visible when people watch the video. Another great way to use affiliate marketing is to provide links and pictures to the links on your website. This helps people visualize the product, which makes them more tempted to purchase it.

One thing that it is very important to remember is that all you need is a person to click on your affiliate link in order to get credit for the sale. What I mean by this is, say a person clicks your link and decides not to purchase the item. Once they have clicked, it takes the person to Amazon and you will get credit for ANY item in their cart that they purchase. For example, during holidays many people had their carts filled with gifts and things for people. If a person happened to click one of our links and checked out, we got a percentage of the sale for the total cart! Therefore, it is extremely important to try and get as many clicks as possible so that you can generate some more passive income.

3. Example of Using Amazon Affiliate

One video that having an Amazon Affiliate link has really paid off is my video, "Frozen Shoulder Physical Therapy Pulley Exercises." This video shows some basic pulley exercises that patients can do for a condition known as "Frozen Shoulder." This is the first half of the description:

Buy on Amazon - https://amzn.to/2Jbj5xM

https://www.PhysicalTherapy101.net - This video

demonstrates several different pulley exercises to treat frozen shoulder. These exercises can also be used after shoulder surgery, manipulation, and for bursitis.

More Information: https://www.physicaltherapy101.net/shoulder/frozen-shoulder-adhesive-capsulitis/

In this description, I have immediately added an Amazon Affiliate link to the pulleys that are being used in the video. This allows the viewer to purchase these if they are interested so that they can follow along exactly at home. The next line is a link to our website and a brief description of the video. The link to our website takes the viewer to the home page where affiliate links are hyperlinked throughout. Finally, the last link takes the viewer directly to the Frozen Shoulder section of my website where the page includes hyperlinks and picture affiliate links to products that will help with Frozen Shoulder. Having these links in the video can potentially lead to more clicks and more affiliate sales.

Final Thoughts

Beginning your YouTube journey can be quite an intimidating one because you are starting something completely new. You may think that it is extremely difficult to pursue and get discouraged however many people are able to accomplish their goals on the YouTube platform. Take it from me, I am a Physical Therapist who was able to create a profitable YouTube Channel. If I am able to accomplish this, then I firmly believe that anybody can do it as long as they put in the effort and implement some of these strategies that leg to my successes so far.

About the Author

Nicholas Gallo is a board certified Doctor of Physical Therapy. He has helped countless patients in his career and continues to practice Physical Therapy on a full time basis. He is also a cofounder of Physical Therapy 101.